GRAMMAR

KEY STAGE 2: Y3–4/ P4–5

MARY PATTINSON

Contents

- Introduction — 3
- Capital letters — 4
- First punctuation — 10
- Nouns — 16
- Adjectives — 22
- Verbs — 28
- Pronouns — 34
- Speech — 40
- Apostrophes — 46
- Sentence length — 52
- Using paragraphs — 58

Published by Hopscotch Educational Publishing Company Ltd, 29 Waterloo Place, Leamington Spa CV32 5LA 01926 744227

© 1998 Hopscotch Educational Publishing

Written by Mary Pattinson
Series design by Blade Communications
Illustrated by Susan Hutchison
Cover illustration by Pat Murray
Printed by Clintplan, Southam

Mary Pattinson hereby asserts her moral right to be identified as the author of this work in accordance with the Copyright, Designs and Patents Act, 1988.

ISBN 1-902239-10-5

All rights reserved. This book is sold subject to the condition that it shall not, by way of trade or otherwise, be lent, hired out or otherwise circulated without the publisher's prior consent in any form or binding or cover other than that in which it is published and without a similar condition, including this condition, being imposed upon the subsequent purchaser.

No part of this publication may be reproduced, stored in a retrieval system, or transmitted, in any form or by any means, electronic, mechanical photocopying, recording or otherwise, without the prior permission of the publisher, except where photocopying for educational purposes within the school or other educational establishment that has purchased this book is expressly permitted in the text.

Introduction

ABOUT THE SERIES

Developing Literacy Skills is a series of books aimed at developing key literacy skills using stories, non-fiction, poetry and rhyme, spelling and grammar, from Key Stage 1 (P1–3) through to Key Stage 2 (P4–7).

The series offers a structured approach which provides detailed lesson plans to teach specific literacy skills. A unique feature of the series is the provision of differentiated photocopiable activities aimed at considerably reducing teacher preparation time. Suggestions for using the photocopiable pages as a stimulus for further work in the classroom is provided to ensure maximum use of this resource.

ABOUT THIS BOOK

This book is for teachers of children at Key Stage 2 Y3–4 and Scottish levels P4–5. It aims to:

✦ develop children's grammar skills through exposure to and experience of a wide range of stimulating texts with supporting differentiated activities which are both diversified and challenging;
✦ support teachers by providing practical teaching methods based on whole-class, group, paired and individual teaching;
✦ encourage enjoyment and curiosity as well as develop skills of interpretation and response.

CHAPTER CONTENT

✦ Overall aims

These outline the aims for both lessons set out in each chapter.

✦ Featured book

This details the children's storybook that could be used in the lessons to support the grammar skill being addressed.

✦ Intended learning

This sets out the specific aims for each individual lesson within the chapter.

✦ Starting point

This provides ideas for introducing the activity and may include key questions to ask the children.

✦ Activity

This explains the task(s) the children will carry out in the lesson without supporting photocopiable activities.

✦ Using the differentiated activity sheets

This explains how to use each sheet as well as providing guidance on the type of child who will benefit most from each sheet.

✦ Plenary session

This suggests ideas for whole-class sessions to discuss the learning outcomes and follow-up work.

✦ Using the photocopiable sheets as a stimulus for further work

This is a useful list of further activities that can be developed from the activity sheets. These ideas maximise the use of the photocopiable pages.

✦ Other ideas for using . . .

This contains other ideas for developing the skills explored in each chapter. The ideas will have completely different learning intentions from the featured lessons and provide a range of alternatives.

And finally . . .

Page 64 contains a list of the children's books which are featured as the basis for developing grammar skills, although other books might be equally valid.

Capital letters

◆ Overall aims

◆ To investigate and be aware of the uses of capitalisation from children's reading.

◆ Featured book

The Suitcase Kid
by Jacqueline Wilson

Story synopsis: When Andy's parents divorce she has to get used to having five and a half step brothers and sisters. Having been an only child she finds her whole life changes. One week she lives with her mum, Bill the Baboon and his three children. The next week she lives with her dad, Carrie and the twins. But all Andy wants is to go home, back to the time when she lived happily with both her mum and her dad in Mulberry Cottage.

◆ Intended learning

◆ To identify and note proper nouns in reading and to use the term 'proper noun'.
◆ To investigate the uses of capitalisation for proper nouns and titles.

◆ Starting point: Whole class

◆ Discuss the plot and the characters. Ask the children the following questions:
Q Why do you think the title is *The Suitcase Kid*?
Q Why do you think each chapter is a letter of the alphabet?
Q What are the names of the characters?
◆ Talk about names. Talk about the children's own names, names they like, names they dislike, nicknames and so on.
◆ Ask someone to write his name on the board. Ask the children why they think it begins with a capital letter. Explain that it is a special name – not just boy or girl, but Joe or Jessica – individual people.
◆ Write on the board the names of the book's characters indicating the capital letters. Ask the children what other words have capital letters – special names, days, months, special occasions. Ask for examples.

◆ Group activities

◆ Divide the class into groups and appoint a scribe. In the story some characters have nicknames, such as Bill Baboon and Andy Pandy. Ask the groups to try to make up nicknames for Katie, Paula, Graham, Carrie, Zen and Crystal. Remind them to think about the person's character or personality in choosing a suitable nickname. Then ask them to imagine the characters all live at different addresses and to suggest appropriate addresses for them. For example, Bill the Baboon may live at Zoo Cottage. Ask the children to try to make the addresses relevant and amusing. Remind them to use capital letters when writing them.

◆ Plenary session

Bring the class together again and discuss with them the nicknames given to the characters. Write some of them on the board indicating where the capital letters should be. Do the same for the addresses. Discuss addressing a letter, setting out an address including where capital letters are required.

Capital letters

✦ LESSON TWO ✦

✦ Intended learning

- To investigate and be aware of capitalisation in headings, titles and abbreviations.
- To remind children that a sentence begins with a capital letter and that the pronoun 'I' is always a capital letter.

✦ Starting point: Whole class

- Review the work of the previous lesson, reminding the class of the need for capital letters when using proper nouns.
- Ask the children to look at the title of *The Suitcase Kid*. Ask which words have capital letters. Look at titles of other books. Do all the words have capital letters? Discuss other titles, such as for films and television programmes.
- Ask the children to suggest other instances when a capital letter is necessary, such as for beginning a sentence, the word 'I' and initials or abbreviations. Discuss how capital letters are used in letters – addresses; Dear . . .; Yours . . . Revise correct setting out of letters.

✦ Using the differentiated activity sheets

Explain to the children that they will have the opportunity of using capital letters in their own writing by writing a letter, like Andy did in the story.

Activity sheet 1

This is aimed at children who need practice in identifying when capital letters need to be used. It also gives scope for personal writing.

Activity sheet 2

This includes a cloze procedure to enable children to write their own words which need capitals as well as giving practice in identifying where capital letters need to be used. It also gives scope for personal writing.

Activity sheet 3

This is aimed at children who are confident in using capital letters in their writing. The task gives the opportunity to write imaginatively and to use capital letters in a variety of situations.

✦ Plenary session

For Activity sheet 1

Write the uncorrected letter on the board and ask a child to put in the capital letters. Do the rest of the class agree with him/her? Remind them why the capital letter is needed in each instance. Ask them why the capital is needed in each instance.

For Activity sheet 2

Ask the children to read aloud the cloze suggestions in their letters. Are they similar? Are they identical? Can the class agree on the best words for the spaces? Again, ask them to read aloud their letter endings. Discuss their use of capital letters.

For Activity sheet 3

Ask the children to read aloud their letters and discuss them with the class. Discuss the use of capital letters.

Capital letters

USING THE PHOTOCOPIABLE SHEETS AS A STIMULUS FOR FURTHER WORK

- Ask the children to respond to the letters as if they were the friend. Discuss with them ideas of what may be included in the reply. This will give further practice in letter writing skills.

- Ask the children to make lists of their favourite films, television programmes or books. Remind them that most conjunctions, prepositions and articles in titles do not have a capital letter, for example *The Lion, the Witch and the Wardrobe*. Make a graph or chart to show the favourites within the class.

- Ask the children to write a review of an evening's television. This could be limited to children's programmes or extended to early evening programmes. This task is suited to group work – each group taking a particular time slot of viewing.

- Ask the children to write character studies for the aunt's sons. What kind of characters are they?

- Write 'real' letters for a 'real' purpose in order to obtain a 'real' response. For example, write to the local council about a local issue /or write to other children in another class or school.

OTHER IDEAS FOR USING CAPITAL LETTERS

- Ask the children to design a poster for a school event, such as a concert or a school fete. Discuss using capital letters for headings and important information on the poster. Remind them also to use capitals for dates and places. This task could also create discussion on sorting important information and highlighting it by varying letter size.

- Play *The Initial Game*. Write down the initials of everyone in the class. Using the initials, the children have to make an adjective and a noun, for example MP – messy puppy. This task gives further practice in the use of adjectives and nouns.

- Ask the children to create their own game of *Happy Families* by making family cards, such as Mr. Diamond the jeweller and Pearl Diamond the jeweller's daughter.

- Ask the children to plan a journey from an atlas. They must write the names of the countries (or towns) they would pass through.

- Play *The Name Game*. In pairs, ask the children to find a boy's and girl's name for every letter of the alphabet. Give a time limit. The winner is the pair with the most names. (Only those with capital letters may be counted!)

- Ask the children to find out about the Standard International Phonetic Alphabet and write it out for display. (Alpha, Bravo, Charlie and so on.)

- Look up abbreviations in dictionaries. Make a collection of them, listing their meanings. Various games may be played using them.

Activity 1   Name _____

◆ My letter ◆

- Imagine you are sick in bed. You decide to write a letter to a friend. This is the beginning of your letter. The capital letters are missing. Put them in and then complete the letter. Remember to use a capital letter at the beginning of sentences and for special names.

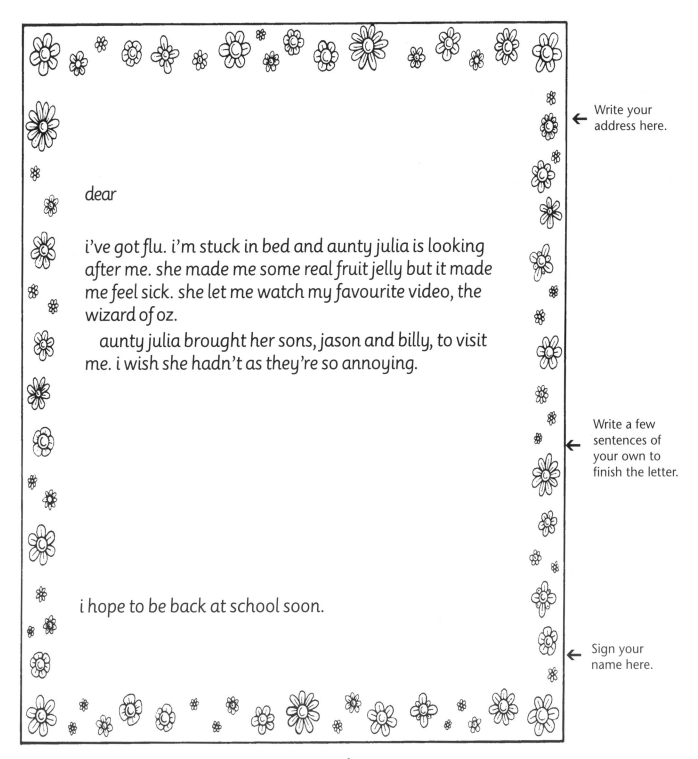

dear

i've got flu. i'm stuck in bed and aunty julia is looking after me. she made me some real fruit jelly but it made me feel sick. she let me watch my favourite video, the wizard of oz.

  aunty julia brought her sons, jason and billy, to visit me. i wish she hadn't as they're so annoying.

i hope to be back at school soon.

← Write your address here.

← Write a few sentences of your own to finish the letter.

← Sign your name here.

Activity 2   Name _____

◆ My letter ◆

✦ Imagine you are sick in bed. You decide to write a letter to a friend. The capital letters are missing. Correct the letter by putting them in. Find suitable words to put in the spaces. Write in your address. This is the beginning of your letter.

---

dear

i'm in bed with flu. my aunty _____ is looking after me. she made me some _____ but it made me feel sick. she let me watch my favourite video, _____.
   aunty julia brought her sons, _____ and _____, to visit me. i really wish i could _____ instead of being sick in bed. did you watch _____ last night? i did. it was really good. i'm reading _____ _____ by _____. it is a good story.

Grammar   Photocopiable

Activity 3 Name _____

◆ My letter ◆

◆ Imagine you are sick in bed. You write a letter to a friend. Write the letter, setting it out correctly. Here are some ideas:

1) Tell your friend what books you are reading, games you are playing and videos you are watching.

2) Tell your friend how you are feeling and who is looking after you.

3) Tell your friend what you would like to do when you get better.

◆ Check that you have used capital letters in the correct places.

First punctuation

Overall aims

- To raise the children's awareness of what makes sentences work.
- To enable children to use, create and respond to different kinds of sentences.
- To emphasise the need for punctuation to aid reading – allowing text to be read aloud with intonation and expression.

Featured book

The Hodgeheg
by Dick King-Smith

Story synopsis: This is the story of Max, the hedgehog who becomes a hodgeheg and a hero. The hedgehog family dream of reaching the park but there is a very busy road to cross. Max knows humans can cross roads quite safely so he determines to find a way for hedgehogs to do the same. He has, however, an unfortunate experience on a zebra crossing which accounts for the spelling of the title of this story.

Intended learning

- To listen to intonation and expression of the text according to the punctuation.
- To write sentences using the correct punctuation to end the sentences.

Starting point: Whole class

- Read to the end of Chapter 3 so that the children can grasp the content. Then read it aloud a second time and ask them to listen for, and indicate, the pauses which demark the sentences. Can they identify the questions in the text? What were the questions asked? Who asks the questions? Who answers them?
- Revise the need for a capital letter to begin a sentence. Demonstrate the three types of punctuation needed to end a sentence (full stop, question mark, exclamation mark) by writing examples on the board. Explain that the punctuation mark shows how the sentence should be read.

Group activities

Divide the children into small groups and appoint a scribe.
- Ask one group to discuss and decide upon five questions they would like to ask Max about his ordeal.
- Another group could make up a sentence about each of the characters in the story. Remind them that names must have a capital letter.
- Others could make up some exclamation sentences that the characters may have said, such as Max – "Ouch! That hurt!" and Cyclist – "Look where you're going!"

Plenary session

Bring the children together to discuss their ideas. Share some of the questions they would put to Max. What were the most common asking or question words? (*What? Where? Why?* and so on.) What other question words can the class find? Discuss the sentences made up about the characters. Make a collaborative character study or description of one of them. Share some of the exclamation sentences and write them on the board with the correct punctuation. Remind the class of the correct punctuation for each sentence type.

First punctuation

◆ LESSON TWO ◆

◆ Intended learning

- To make sense of strings of words by adding appropriate gaps between words and adding punctuation to form sentences.
- To identify statements, exclamations and questions and use the correct punctuation.

◆ Starting point: Whole class

- Remind the children of the previous lesson and revise the need for sentences to begin with capital letters and end with a full stop, exclamation mark or question mark.
- Find examples of statements, exclamations and questions from *The Hodgeheg* to read aloud to the children. Can they tell you how the sentence would be punctuated at the end?
- Share a prepared large text where there are no gaps in between the words, for example:
thissentencedoesnothaveanygapsinbetweenthewordswhichmakesitverydifficulttoread
(this sentence does not have any gaps in between the words which makes it very difficult to read)
- Ask the children to try and decipher the sentence. Discuss the importance of having gaps in between words and a clearly defined beginning and end to each sentence.
- Have fun by asking them to write a statement, exclamation or question sentence without any gaps in between the words. Ask them to try and see if a partner can decipher the text.
- Explain that they will now have an opportunity to decipher some more text and write their own statement, exclamation and question sentences.

◆ Using the differentiated activity sheets

Activity sheet 1

This is aimed at those children who may need visual support to decode the sentences. The sentences are separated for them so the children need only concentrate on capital letters and the correct sentence punctuation at the end.

Activity sheet 2

This requires the children to sort the text into sentences as well as add the capitals and punctuation.

Activity sheet 3

This is more challenging in that it requires the children to proof read the text and decide on the correct punctuation to use.

◆ Plenary session

Bring the whole class together again when the children have completed the tasks. Discuss any problems they may have had in deciding where to place word gaps or what punctuation to use. Is the text easier to read once the punctuation is included? Share some of the children's own sentences from each activity. Write some of them up and ask the children to punctuate them.

Grammar
KS2: Y3–4/P4–5

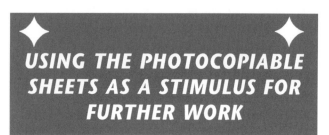

First punctuation

USING THE PHOTOCOPIABLE SHEETS AS A STIMULUS FOR FURTHER WORK

OTHER IDEAS FOR FIRST PUNCTUATION

◆ Activity sheet 1

- Provide the children with slips of paper with statement, question and exclamation sentences written on them. Ask them to sort the sentences into the relevant boxes or under relevant headings indicated by punctuation marks ! . ?
- Share the questions the children have written about road safety. In groups, ask them to write the answers to the questions. Make them up into a class road safety book.
- In enlarged text, write out some sentences without word gaps. Ask the children to cut out the words to make sentences. Use this activity to discuss word order possibilities.

◆ Activity sheet 2

- Ask the children to write their own short text without gaps and punctuation. Challenge a partner to decipher it.
- Provide the children with muddled sentences from *The Hodgeheg* and ask them to unscramble them. Use this time to discuss the importance of the order of words in sentences.

◆ Activity sheet 3

- Ask the children to write out some sentences by writing each word on a separate piece of card. Can a partner make up the sentence using the words? How many different sentences can be made using the same words?
- Make a class road safety book using the questions and answers from the activity sheet.
- Ask the children to write road safety poems using statements, exclamations and questions.

- In groups play *Who is it?* One member of the group thinks of a famous person. The others try to guess his identity. Each child must use a different asking word, such as *What...? How...? When..?* The children are limited to one question each. The child who finds the correct answer has the opportunity of choosing the next personality.

- Create a class collection of Knock! Knock! jokes to practise using questions and statements.

- Interviews. Working in pairs the children conduct verbal role play interviews. This may take the form of radio/television interviews or for magazines/newspapers.

- The last activity may be extended to the children interviewing real people outside the classroom. Written questions may be prepared for this activity.

- The children could make up games of consequences in which certain questions are asked, an answer written, hidden from view and passed on to the next person. This person then adds his answer to the next question and so on. This can make amusing reading.

Activity 1 Name _____

◆ Road safety ◆

◆ Look at these pictures of Sam trying to cross a busy road.
   Work out what you think the text says underneath each picture.

samtriestocrosstheroad

alorrynearlyrunsoverhim

samtriestocrossagain

acarnearlyhitshim

samwalkstothezebracrossing

whydidn'thecrossherefirst

◆ Write out the six story sentences correctly. Remember to use capital letters, full stops, exclamation marks and question marks.

1 _____
2 _____
3 _____
4 _____
5 _____
6 _____

◆ Now use the back of this page to write four sentences of your own about road safety. Include a question and an exclamation in your sentences.

Grammar
KS2: Y3–4/P4–5

Activity 2 Name _____

◆ Road safety ◆

✦ Read the following passage to yourself. It is about a boy called Sam.

samwantedtocrossthebusyroadinhistowntogototheshophetriedtocrossataplace withoutazebracrossingandhewasnearlyhitbyalorryandthenbyacarsamdecided thatitwastoodangeroustocrossatthisplacesohewalkedtothenearestzebracrossing whenheusedthecrossinghewassafelyacrosstheroadinnotimeatall

✦ Did you find this difficult to read? Write out the passage again with gaps in between the words. Remember to use capital letters and full stops.

_____
_____
_____
_____
_____
_____
_____

✦ When Sam returned home, his mother asked him about his trip to the shop. Here are the answers Sam gave. Make up the questions his mother may have asked to match the answers.

Q _____

A No, I didn't use the zebra crossing at first.

Q _____

A I thought it might be quicker to cross right opposite the shop.

Q _____

A Next time I'm going to use the crossing!

Activity 3   **Name** _____

◆ Road safety ◆

◆ In the passage below, the punctuation is muddled. Re-write it putting in the capital letters and full stops in the correct places so that it makes sense.

sam decided to go to the shop he. was in a hurry so he tried to cross right opposite. the Shop he stepped out onto the Road. and a huge Lorry nearly hit him Sam. stepped out onto the road again and a Car forced him to Step back. on the footpath. This frightened sam so he decided to walk to the Nearest Zebra. crossing here he Safely crossed. the road in no time at all

_____
_____
_____
_____
_____
_____

◆ Sam decides to warn other children about the dangers of crossing the road. He writes a question and answer book and puts it in the school library. Think up some questions and answers for Sam's road safety book. Write them here.

Remember to use capital letters, full stops, question marks and exclamation marks where necessary.

_____
_____
_____
_____
_____
_____

Grammar

Nouns

 Overall aims

- To identify nouns as naming words and to use the term 'noun' when discussing them.
- To investigate patterns of puralisation in words.
- To understand the terms 'singular' and 'plural'.
- To understand the meaning of collective nouns and to identify, invent and collect examples of them.

 Featured book

The Better Brown Stories
by Allan Ahlberg

Story synopsis: The subjects of this book, the Brown family, are not happy with the way the writer portrays them, so they visit the writer and ask him to include them in more exciting and adventurous tales. Little do they know what is in store for them! A monstrous milkman, an enormous dog, free money and some mysterious men all contribute to make this a marvellous and original story.

 Intended learning

- To identify nouns as 'naming' words.
- To help children understand the meaning of collective nouns and to experiment with inventing and collecting examples of them.

 Starting point: Whole class

- Discuss with the class the characters and the plot. Introduce the concept of 'naming' words. Explain that these 'naming' words are called 'nouns'.
- Read Chapter 1 in which the dissatisfied Brown family want things. What do they want? Ask the children to listen to the text and try to identify these things (nouns). Explain to the children that a way of identifying a noun is to put either *a*, *an*, or *the* in front of it. If it makes sense then it is probably a noun, for example (a) book, (an) apple, (the) television. But 'eat' is not a noun because the rule does not apply.
- Put a selection of words on the board and ask the children to use the rule to practise identifying common nouns.
- Introduce the term 'collective noun'. Discuss the fact that collective nouns name a group or collection of something. Ask the class to suggest some collective nouns they are familiar with, for example a flock of sheep. Tell the children the names of other collective nouns.

 Group activities

- Divide the children into groups and play a memory game. 'I went to the writer and I asked for . . .' The first child suggests something that the Brown family asked for, such as more pocket money. The next player repeats the sentence adding another item to the list. Extend this to items the children would ask for if they were in the story. Each child adds a noun to the list until their memory takes them no further.
- Ask the children to invent some collective nouns for the following jobs, all taken from the first chapter in the book: postmen, milkmen, vicars, bank managers, teachers, bakers, fishermen, writers. For example, 'a parcel of postmen'.

 Plenary session

Bring the class together again to share their ideas. What is the longest list remembered by any one group? Ask the groups to share their ideas of the collective nouns they have invented. Which do they think are the most suitable? Write on the board some of the invented 'job' sentences. Does the class find them amusing? Discuss other categories of collective nouns which could be invented, such as food – pizzas, sandwiches, hamburgers and so on.

Nouns

USING THE PHOTOCOPIABLE SHEETS AS A STIMULUS FOR FURTHER WORK

Activity sheet 1

- In pairs, ask the children to make up their own wordsearches related to the story. The partner finds the answers.
- Ask the children to try making up wordsearches with plural nouns.

Activity sheet 2

- Change the nouns in the word DOG from singular to plural. Which nouns follow the pattern of simply adding 's'? Which words have to change their spelling? Which word remains the same in the singular and the plural?
- Create more specific function machines, for example change *y* to *ie* and add *s*. This will give practice in plural patterns.
- Reverse some of the functions so that plurals are made into singular nouns.

Activity sheet 3

- Use the nouns in the crossword. Find the singular or plural form of the noun as appropriate. Which word does not change?
- Give sentences in which the noun and verb do not agree. Ask the children to change the sentences to make sense (agreement).

OTHER IDEAS FOR USING NOUNS

- Play *I Spy* games to name classroom objects. Write the items on a sheet of paper in a list. Add the plural of each noun.
- Play *The Naming Game*. Each child has a sheet of paper headed with various categories, such as animal, vegetable, fruit and tree. A letter is chosen and the children have to write as many objects as they can in each category beginning with that letter. A time limit is sensible.
- Play *The Matchbox Game*. Ask the children to collect as many different items as possible to fit into a matchbox. These should be listed and the plurals written beside them. The child with the biggest collection is the winner. (This game is ideal for a fund-raising sponsored event.)
- Give the children a short story with the nouns removed and a silly word in their place, such as *banana(s)*. Ask the children to re-write the story giving suitable nouns in place of *bananas*.

Activity 1   Name _____

◆ Nouns wordsearch ◆

✦ Complete the wordsearch to find the ten items Ben found in the Enormous Dog. To find the nouns, look across, up, down and diagonally. Circle the words as you find them.

P	J	O	Y	S	T	I	C	K	L	T	R
R	H	D	Z	M	B	N	V	W	N	Y	C
O	I	I	D	O	X	J	I	U	B	O	L
O	V	A	W	N	U	P	D	F	G	O	B
D	E	L	X	O	T	T	E	S	S	Y	O
P	N	R	A	B	C	T	O	D	I	F	G
A	O	Z	Y	X	I	W	S	X	A	F	V
R	H	N	O	P	P	Q	C	R	S	T	U
T	P	M	K	L	K	J	R	E	V	E	L
H	I	C	J	K	L	M	E	N	O	P	Q
N	O	N	N	A	C	R	E	T	A	W	R
C	S	T	U	V	N	W	N	X	Y	Z	A

COCKPIT
KNOB
WATER CANNON
FAX
JOYSTICK
LEVER
TRAPDOOR
VIDEO SCREEN
DIAL
PHONE

✦ Now complete the following noun sums:

one bowl + one bowl = _____

one dog + one dog = _____

one dish + one dish = _____

one baby + one baby = _____

three stories − two stories = _____

✦ Now make up some noun sums of your own.

Grammar
KS2: Y3–4/P4–5

Photocopiable
©Hopscotch Educational Publishing
19

Activity 3   Name _____

◆ Nouns crossword ◆

◆ Complete the crossword. All your answers should be nouns. Use a dictionary to help you.

Clues Across
1. Where the pilot sits in a plane.
6. A decayed building.
7. Someone with no home or money who moves from place to place.
8. A young dog.
9. It can be full of clouds.
10. Used to talk to people over long distances.
11. Used to cut food.

Clues Down
1. A name for cows, bulls or oxen.
2. A group of children at school.
3. A red wildflower.
4. A hinged door in a floor.
5. A large town which usually has a cathedral.
10. An abbreviation for Physical Education.

◆ Rewrite this sentence changing all the singular nouns to plurals.

The shed was green and had a door and a window in the side.

_____

◆ Now change the plural nouns to singular.

There were rugs on the floor and photographs, posters and children's letters on the walls.

_____

_____

Grammar — Photocopiable

Adjectives

 ### Overall aims

- To develop children's ability to use language effectively.
- To enable them to gain an understanding of how words work in sentences.
- To encourage them to collect and use describing words and to use the term adjective in relation to them.

 ### Featured book

The Hobbit
by J R R Tolkien

Story synopsis: The Hobbit, Bilbo Baggins is enjoying a life of comfort and contentment in his home in The Hill but his peaceful life changes when Gandalf, the wizard, arrives on his doorstep looking for someone to share in an adventure. Bilbo finds himself joining a party of 13 dwarfs on a quest for dragon-guarded gold. Encounters with giant spiders, evil goblins and dangerous dragons abound until the story reaches its dramatic climax.
Note This is an excellent story to read aloud, but some vocabulary may require explanation.

 ### Intended learning

- To encourage children to explore and appreciate the use of adjectives in figurative language and link it to fiction.
- To encourage them to collect and use describing words and to use the term 'adjective'.

 ### Starting point: Whole class

- Read the opening pages of Chapter 1 in which the author describes the Hobbit and his home. Ask the following questions:

Q How would you describe Bilbo's home?
Q What is your home like? Can you describe it?
Q How does the author let us know that Bilbo lives in some comfort?
Q Do describing words make it easier to imagine what something is like?
Q Do you think the description of the Hobbit's home is a good one?

- Introduce the term 'adjectives' for words describing nouns.
- Explain by writing examples on the board that adjectives often come immediately before the noun they are describing – Bilbo lived in a comfortable home. But they can also be some way from the noun – Bilbo lived in a home in The Hill which was very comfortable.
- Give examples of how, by changing an adjective, the whole image of a sentence can alter. For example, The dog barked loudly. The fierce dog barked loudly. The excited dog barked loudly.
- Remind them that colours are adjectives.

 ### Group activities

- Each group should 'brainstorm' adjectives to describe a Hobbit. If necessary, guide them by suggesting the following: What was his face like? Did he have hair? What about his feet? and so on.
- Using their ideas, ask the groups to produce a labelled picture of a Hobbit, showing as much detail as possible.

 ### Plenary session

Display the pictures and compare them. Are they alike in any way? This task could be an opportunity to introduce comparison of adjectives. For example, This Hobbit has big ears. This one has bigger ears but this one has the biggest. Discuss the variety of adjectives used. Can they be improved? Are there better words than 'big'? Read again Tolkien's description of the Hobbit. How do the children's views compare? Remind them that the use of adjectives gives greater interest to writing.

Adjectives

LESSON TWO

Intended learning

- To develop children's ability to use language effectively by understanding how an adjective works in a sentence.
- To explore ways of predicting, substituting and adding adjectives in sentences.

Starting point: Whole class

- Review the work covered in the previous lesson. Revise the part of the story where Bilbo meets Gandalf and Gandalf explains that he is looking for someone to share in an adventure. Ask the following questions:
- Q What do you think about the author's description of Gandalf? Is it interesting? Exciting?
- Q Are we told what Gandalf is like as a person or just what he looks like?
- Q What sort of person do you think he is?
- Q Why do you think that the author does not let the reader know too much about Gandalf?

Using the differentiated activity sheets

Explain to the children that they will have the opportunity of using adjectives to make their own descriptions of a wizard.

Activity sheet 1

This is aimed at children who may need visual support to describe nouns. They are initially given a choice of words to complete the task. The second task encourages them to make their own choices.

Activity sheet 2

This is aimed at children who are able to work more independently and are capable of recognising adjectives.

Activity sheet 3

This is aimed at children who are much more confident in their ability to use adjectives correctly in sentences. It is intended to expand their vocabulary and further their writing skills.

Plenary session

For Activity sheet 1
Ask someone to read out his adjectives/nouns for the wizard. Do the others agree? Could other words be substituted? Ask someone to read out their cloze description of the wizard. Does it make sense? Could it be improved in any way?

For Activity sheet 2
Ask someone to read the original description of the wizard. Does it make sense? Could any of the adjectives remain in the same place? Ask someone to read the revised version. Does this give a better picture of the wizard? Ask the children to show their pictures. Compare them with the picture on Activity sheet 1. Are they similar in any way?

For Activity sheet 3
Ask some of these children to read their list of adjectives.

Read some descriptions aloud and discuss the adjectives used. Could any of these be improved by substituting better adjectives?

Adjectives

USING THE PHOTOCOPIABLE SHEETS AS A STIMULUS FOR FURTHER WORK

Activity sheet 1

- Take the first task one stage further by suggesting the children add two adjectives to the noun, such as a 'blue pointed hat'.
- Discuss with the children where the wizard might live. Use adjectives to describe his house in detail.
- Ask the children to write a story about the wizard.

Activity sheet 2

- Find synonyms for the adjectives. Encourage the use of a thesaurus.
- Create a word bank of adjectives for story-writing.
- Ask the children to suggest antonyms for the adjectives underlined, for example patterned – plain.

Activity sheet 3

- Ask the children to use a thesaurus to find as many different adjectives as they can for the ones they have used.
- Ask the children to make up their own spells which the wizard might use. They should use as many adjectives as possible to describe their ingredients and the effect of the spell.
- Challenge the children to find antonyms for their adjectives.

OTHER IDEAS FOR USING ADJECTIVES

- The children sit in a circle. The first child says a noun to his neighbour, such as 'book'. The neighbour then has to think of a suitable adjective to go with the noun, for example 'exciting'. The next person has to add a different noun to the adjective, such as 'game' and so on. Encourage a wide range of adjectives and nouns.

- Make up an alphabetical list of adjectives by playing a game based on 'I went to the shops and I bought . . . an appetising apple, a boring book' and so on.

- Working in pairs, each child draws a 'Wanted' portrait. They must not let their partner see their portrait. They take it in turns to describe their drawing to their partner who then has to draw the character from the description given. The two are compared for likeness. Emphasise the need for adjectival detail to produce an accurate portrait. For example, he has a long, curved scar below his left eye.

- Give the children a 'nice' story – a short story in which almost every adjective is 'nice'. For example: Once upon a time there lived a nice girl who lived in a nice house by a nice stream . . . Ask the children to rewrite the story substituting better adjectives for the word 'nice'.

- Ask the children to collect advertisements from newspapers and magazines. Discuss the language used by the advertisers. What adjectives do they use? For example, More! Better! Larger! Why are these words used? Create group or individual advertisements for an imaginary product. Encourage the children to think about persuasive language.

Activity 1 Name _____

✦ The wizard ✦

✦ Choose adjectives from the box to complete the labels.

pointed   long
patterned
bushy   huge
wooden

✦ Colour the picture. Write a colour adjective for the following:

a _____ hat

a _____ beard

a _____ scarf

a _____ cloak

_____ boots

a _____ stick

✦ Now write adjectives of your choice in the spaces below.

The wizard is a _____ man with a _____ stick.

He is wearing _____ clothes and speaks in a _____

voice. When he laughs his eyes are _____ and when he

frowns his eyes are _____ .

Grammar
KS2: Y3–4/P4–5

Activity 2   Name _____

◆ The wizard ◆

◆ Here is a description of a wizard but the adjectives are muddled. Rewrite it by putting the adjectives in the correct places.

The wizard is an black man with a very patterned beard which reaches below his waist. His hat is bushy and long with a tall brim. He wears a pointed cloak and enormous shady boots. His old eyebrows stick out to the sides of his hat.

_____
_____
_____
_____
_____

◆ Use this description to draw a picture. Colour your picture and give the wizard a blue hat and a grey cloak.

◆ Write some more adjectives to describe a wizard. Use a dictionary or a thesaurus to help you.

Grammar   Photocopiable
KS2: Y3–4/P4–5   ©Hopscotch Educational Publishing

Activity 3

◆ The wizard ◆

✦ Draw a picture of a wizard.

✦ Use a dictionary to help you write adjectives to describe the wizard.

Other adjectives that might describe a wizard.

magical	mysterious
solitary	secretive
charismatic	spellbinding
imposing	impressive
powerful	splendid

✦ Use some of the adjectives in the box as well as your own to write a very detailed description of the wizard. Describe what he looks like, the clothes he is wearing and how he lives and behaves. Use a thesaurus to find the best descriptive words.

Continue on the back of this sheet.

Verbs

◆ Overall aims

- To develop the children's ability to use language effectively.
- To enable children to identify verbs as action words in sentences and to link them to reading.
- To give them an understanding of the term 'tense' (that it refers to time) in relation to verbs.
- To investigate verb tenses – past, present and future.

◆ Featured book

The Iron Man
by Ted Hughes

Story synopsis: A huge iron giant topples from a cliff and is smashed and scattered on the rocks below. His various parts get up and search for each other and he proceeds to devour all metal machinery in his path. A menace to the local farmers, it is decided that the Iron Man must be stopped. A trap is set and the giant is captured, but the farmers reckon without the Iron Man's determination to be free!

◆ LESSON ONE ◆

◆ Intended learning

- To examine the work of the action words in a sentence and begin to use the term 'verb' appropriately.
- To collect, classify and use a range of similar or synonymous verbs, creating families of verbs.

◆ Starting point: Whole class

- Read the first two chapters of the book to the class. Discuss the language used and the plot. Explain to the children that the things that happen – the action words – are verbs. Read examples of action words from the book which describe the Iron Man's movements. Ask the children to name actions that their own bodies can do. For example, What can you do with your hand? – wave, clap, stroke and so on. Use the term 'verb' in relation to these actions.
- Build up a class bank of body action words – this can be visual, for example a large drawing of an Iron Man to fill with suitable verbs.
- Write examples on the board of action sentences but omit the verb, for example The Iron man over the cliff. (tumbled)
- Ask the children – Does it make sense? What words could be used to correct the sentence? Explain that a sentence needs a verb to give it sense.

◆ Group activities

Divide the children into groups. Each group needs access to a thesaurus. Appoint a scribe.
- Synonymous verbs – Ask the children to collect alternative verbs for the verbs in sentences, such as: The Iron Man *came* to a cliff. He *fell* over the cliff. His eye and hand *got* together. Ask them to list as many alternative words for 'came' as possible – arrived at, climbed, reached and so on. Encourage them to use a thesaurus. They should check that the sentence still makes sense when a replacement verb is used.

◆ Plenary session

Bring the class together to discuss the synonyms for 'came', 'fell' and 'got'. Play *The Synonym Game*; ask the scribe to read out their alternative verbs for 'came'. If none of the other groups has found the same word, two points are awarded to the group. If another group has the same word, then one point is awarded. The group with the most unusual list of verbs should gain the most points and win the game. Do the same with 'fell' and 'got' if time allows. Ask the children for suggestions as to how to use these synonyms to improve their own writing.

Verbs

◆ LESSON TWO ◆

✦ Intended learning

- To identify verbs as action words in sentences.
- To build confidence in using a variety of verbs in own writing.
- To develop an awareness of how tense relates to purpose and structure of text.

✦ Starting point: Whole class

- Read Chapter 3 of *The Iron Man*. Discuss what tenses mean and ask the children to tell you what tense the story is written in. Explain that most narratives are written in the past tense. Ask the children why this might be.
- Read a short recipe or set of instructions to the class. What tense is used? Why is the present tense used for these types of text?
- Introduce the concept of tense relating to time. The class timetable would be a practical way to explain this. For example, Yesterday we *had* History. Today we *have* Science. Tomorrow we *will have* PE. Ask the children for further examples.

✦ Using the differentiated activity sheets

Activity sheet 1

This requires the children to use their own verbs to complete the sentences. Examples of changes in tense within word families are given.

Activity sheet 2

This requires the children to recognise verbs in sentences and to change verbs from present to past tense.

Activity sheet 3

This is more challenging because it requires the children to use notes to write a report in the past tense.

✦ Plenary session

When the children have completed their tasks, bring the whole class together again.

For Activity sheet 1
Ask a child to explain what they had to do and to read out their sentences. Stop at each verb and ask others to tell you what other verbs could be used so the sentence still makes sense. Discuss the correct tense to use – the passage is in the past tense – are the examples given also in the past tense? Ask a child to read out his word families. Which words do not follow the same pattern as the others?

For Activity sheet 2
Ask one child to read out the passage. What tense is used? Ask another child to read out the same passage in the past tense. Ask everyone to listen carefully to see if the tenses used are correct.

For Activity sheet 3
Ask one child to read out their newspaper article. Are verbs used in the heading? What impact do they have? Are newspaper articles always in the past tense? Why?

Grammar
KS2: Y3–4/P4–5

Verbs

USING THE PHOTOCOPIABLE SHEETS AS A STIMULUS FOR FURTHER WORK

Activity sheet 1

- Investigate some common endings of verbs, such as –ed, –ing. Ask the children to investigate whether there is any connection between the endings and the tense of a verb.
- The opening of the book says that nobody knew where the Iron Man had come from or how he was made. Ask the children to:
  – write a prequel to the story answering these questions. (past tense)
  – write some instructions for making an Iron Man. Give suggestions of different items of machinery that could be used. (present tense)

Activity sheet 2

- Rewrite the first passage replacing the verbs with alternatives. These could be synonyms or entirely different verbs which may alter the meaning of the text.
- Using the same passage, ask the children to write the negative version of the verbs. For example, the spaceship did not hover . . .
- Ask the children to create word families from the verbs on this sheet.

Activity sheet 3

- Using examples from newspapers, discuss with the children the style of writing reports.
- Look at how verbs in a newspaper article give meaning to the report.
- Discuss how a different slant could be given to a report by altering the verbs.
- Discuss how verbs could be used to create sensationalism in a report.
- Change the passage on the sheet to the future tense.

OTHER IDEAS FOR USING VERBS

- Working in groups. One member mimes an action. The others in turn must try to guess the action. This could be developed into a *What's My Line?* type of game in which the children mime actions associated with jobs.

- The children are given a written passage in which the verbs have been replaced by nonsense verbs. This makes the text quite amusing. The task is to replace the nonsense verbs with others appropriate to the text.

- Poetry at the simplest level. Ask the children to create a two word animal poem. Each line has a subject and a verb only, for example Tigers roar. Encourage the children to find more and more interesting verbs. This could be developed according to their ability.

- The children are given a written passage in which the verbs have been removed entirely. Ask the children to work in pairs to suggest a suitable verb to be put in the correct place in the sentence.

- Ask the children to make an alphabetical list of verbs, such as arguing, bumping and crawling.

- Make up a word bank of onomatopoeic words – splash! crash!

- Ask the children to compose simple crosswords consisting entirely of verbs.

Activity 1 Name _____

✦ The Alien ✦

✦ Read the text below about an alien arriving on Earth. Write verbs in the spaces so that the sentences make sense.

The spaceship _____ above the ground for a little while, then it _____. A huge door slowly _____ and a bright light _____ out. Some steps _____ and a strange creature _____ down them. The alien moved with a clanging sound. It _____ around and then _____ down the hill to the lake. Suddenly, a man _____ and shouted at the alien. Quickly, the alien <u>clanged</u>, <u>rattled</u>, <u>banged</u> and <u>jerked</u> its way back to the spaceship.

The words clanged, rattled, banged and jerked are underlined because these are the actions the alien made when it moved.

✦ In the box below, write some other action words to show how the alien might have moved. Use a dictionary to help you.

[   ]

✦ Find the word families for these action words. The first one has been done for you.

crashes	bumps	topples
	break	tumble
bumped	tumbling	toppled
	bumping	crashed
tumbled	breaking	broke
	toppling	crashing

1 <u>crashes   crashed   crashing</u>
2 _____
3 _____
4 _____
5 _____

Grammar
KS2: Y3–4/P4–5

Photocopiable

31

©Hopscotch Educational Publishing

Activity 2 Name _____

◆ The Alien ◆

✦ Underline all the verbs in this passage about an alien. There are 14 verbs to find. Fit them into the puzzle.

The magnificent spaceship hovers above the ground. I see bright lights shining from it in all directions. Without a sound, the spaceship lands on the grass. A large door slides open and some huge steps appear. There at the top of the steps stands a weird creature. The alien slowly judders down the steps, making strange sounds. It clangs, rattles, bangs and jerks its way to the lake where it disappears from my sight.

✦ All these verbs above are in the present tense. In the box below, re-write the passage and change all the verbs to the past tense.

Activity 3   Name _____

◆ The Alien ◆

✦ Imagine you are a newspaper reporter. You have just witnessed the arrival of an alien on Earth. Use the notes below to write your report. Make sure your report is written in sentences with the **verbs** in the **past tense**.

- magnificent spaceship lands near Greenfly Wood
- bright lights shine out
- door slides open
- huge steps roll down
- weird creature appears
- alien is tall, green, with red eyes
- robotic body with wheels on tail
- alien makes strange movements (clangs, rattles, bangs and jerks)
- alien moves to nearby lake
- drinks water from lake
- moves quickly back to spaceship
- spaceship flies off

Daily Herald — 25p

Write your heading here →

Write your article in columns here →

Grammar

KS2: Y3–4/P4–5

Photocopiable

©Hopscotch Educational Publishing

Pronouns

◆ Overall aims

- To identify and note common pronouns in reading, experiment with substituting them in sentences and to use the term 'pronoun'.
- To understand the difference between singular and plural pronouns, such as I/we, me/us, and to use the correct person/verb agreement.
- To identify differences between 1st and 3rd person and to compare and transform sentences.

◆ Featured book

The BFG
by Roald Dahl

Story synopsis: Sophie is snatched from her bed in the middle of the night by a huge giant. She imagines she will be eaten for the giant's breakfast but instead she finds herself with a giant much kinder and much nicer than his neighbours in Giant Country. The other giants enjoy guzzling and swallowing people from all over the world but the Big Friendly Giant just enjoys catching nice dreams and giving them to people. Sophie and the BFG hatch a plan to rid the world of horrid giants.

◆ Intended learning

- To identify common pronouns and understand the term 'pronoun'.
- To understand the difference between singular and plural pronouns.

◆ Starting point: Whole class

- Talk about the way the BFG speaks. Are the words he uses real words? For example, bundongle, whopsy whiffling, scrumdiddlyumptious. Does the reader know what they mean? Why does the author use words like these? Is this vocabulary amusing?
- Read a short passage from the story using the noun each time in place of the pronoun. How does it sound? Is it clumsy? Explain that using pronouns makes speaking and writing much quicker and clearer. Re-read the passage using the pronouns. Ask the class to listen for the difference and ask which they prefer.
- Use the board to illustrate the use of the pronoun so that the children can identify with the written pronoun. For example, write some sentences without pronouns and ask the class to suggest some which could be used in place of the nouns.
- Use the common singular pronouns – *he, she, it, I, me, her, him, you*. And their plurals – *they, we, us, them, you*.

◆ Group activities

- Ask the class to work in pairs. Ask them to imagine they are the BFG. Each child is to write a short passage entitled 'All About Me'. They may write about the BFG's family, his friends, his pets, his home and so on. They must write in the first person. Ask them to include as many of the 12 common pronouns as possible.
- When they have completed the task the partner reads the work and underlines all the pronouns checking that they are correct.

◆ Plenary session

Bring the class together and ask children to read aloud their descriptions 'All About Me'. Discuss the content of the descriptions and ask them to indicate which pronouns have been used. Use the board to make a list. Discuss which pronouns are singular and which are plural. Ensure the children are aware of the difference. Remind them of the job of the pronoun in a sentence.

Pronouns

LESSON TWO

Intended learning

- To understand the purpose of pronouns and to substitute them in sentences.
- To understand the difference between singular and plural pronouns and to use the correct verb agreement.

Starting point: Whole class

- Review the work of the previous lesson reminding the class of the purpose of pronouns in writing and speaking. Continue reading *The BFG* asking the class to be aware of how pronouns are used. Ask the children to consider how the BFG says his sentences. Give some examples, such as 'I is a friendly Giant. I is a nice and jumbly Giant.' Discuss whether this is correct English. How would the children correct these sentences? Ask why they think the author used incorrect language for the giant. Read a passage from the book in which the giant is speaking. Ask the children to indicate when they hear incorrect verb agreement.

Using the differentiated activity sheets

Activity sheet 1

This is aimed at children who need practice in recognising/identifying pronouns in their reading.

Activity sheet 2

This is aimed at children who are more confident in identifying and using pronouns and are able to work independently on pronoun/verb agreement exercises.

Activity sheet 3

This is aimed at children who can confidently identify confidently common pronouns and are more easily able to identify writing with the correct pronoun/ verb agreement.

Plenary session

For Activity sheet 1
Ask one child to read his/her sentences with his chosen pronouns. Ask the class: Do they make sense? Does everyone agree with his choice? Read out some of the sentences using incorrect verb agreement, such as 'Many of the giants is huge . . .' Discuss why the verb agreement is not right.

For Activity sheet 2
Ask one child to show his or her completed grid and then read the sentences with the correct pronoun in place. Discuss with the class why each pronoun is used. Discuss the reasons for the correct verb agreement changes in the three sentences.

For Activity sheet 3
Ask a child to list the 12 pronouns. Ask another child to read the corrected versions of the sentences. Discuss why these changes are necessary.

Pronouns

USING THE PHOTOCOPIABLE SHEETS AS A STIMULUS FOR FURTHER WORK

◆ Activity sheet 1

- Ask the children to decide which pronouns in the giant's cloak are plural and which are singular.

- Using the sentences, change the pronouns from singular to plural and vice-versa where appropriate. For example, The giants ran very fast and they soon caught up with Mary.

- Ask the children to imagine they are chased by a giant and then suggest they write a story about what happens. Remind the children they need to use the first person 'I'.

◆ Activity sheet 2

- Ask the children to imagine they are the giant and write the passage in the first person instead of the third. For example, 'I chased after Mary because . . .'

- Make up sentences which describe Mary and the giant. For example, Mary is . . .; The giant is . . .; They are . . .

◆ Activity sheet 3

- Ask the children to rewrite the passage as if they were Mary. They must write in the first person – 'I ran very fast through the woods . . .'

- Ask the children to find sentences in *The BFG* that use incorrect English. Challenge them to rewrite them using correct English.

OTHER IDEAS FOR USING PRONOUNS

- Make further use of first/third person writing. Discuss with the class what types of text are written in first person – diaries, eye witness reports, autobiographies and so on. And discuss those written in third person – most narratives. Ask the children to write examples of these. Which do they prefer to write? Stress the importance of keeping to the same 'person' throughout their own writing.

- Work with the children on the correct use of 'I' and 'me' in their writing, since the concept is difficult for many children to grasp and these terms are often misused.

- Give the children practice in correct usage by multiple choice exercises, such as Should it be: 'John and me are going to the cinema' or 'John and I are going to the cinema.'? Remember to teach the children to split the sentence to see if it makes sense – 'John is going to the cinema.'; 'Me am going to the cinema.' and 'I am going to the cinema.' Which sounds correct? So 'John and I are going to the cinema' is the correct version.

- If the class is ready to understand new types of pronoun, introduce the possessive pronoun – *mine, yours, his, hers, theirs, its* and *ours*. Give many examples and exercises for the children to gain experience in using them. Cloze exercises and multiple choice questions give good practice in their use.

Activity 1

Name _____

◆ The giant ◆

✦ Copy these sentences. Choose pronouns from the giant's cloak to replace the underlined words.

they   he   she   them   me   her

1. The giant ran very fast and <u>the giant</u> soon caught up with Mary.

2. The girl thought that <u>the giant</u> would eat <u>the girl</u>.

3. "Please don't eat <u>Mary</u>," said Mary.

4. The giant was very friendly so <u>the giant</u> did not eat <u>Mary</u>.

5. "I thought all giants were mean," <u>Mary</u> said.

6. "<u>Giants</u> are often friendly like me," <u>the giant</u> said.

7. So Mary and the giant became friends and <u>Mary and the giant</u> had many adventures together.

Grammar
KS2: Y3-4/P4-5

Photocopiable
©Hopscotch Educational Publishing

Activity 2 Name _____

◆ The giant ◆

◆ Choose pronouns from the giant's cloak to complete the grid below:

	h	e	
	h	e	
	h	e	
	h	e	
	h	e	

◆ Re-write the following using pronouns from the giant's cloak so that each sentence makes better sense.

The giant began to chase after Mary but the giant could not catch up with Mary for quite some time. Mary began to get tired so Mary sat down to rest.
   "Please don't hurt Mary," Mary said to the giant. "Mary am very tired!"
   "The giant won't hurt you," the giant said. "Mary look very tired."
The giant and Mary began to talk. The giant and Mary became good friends.

_____
_____
_____
_____

◆ These sentences are incorrect. Re-write them using correct English.

   1   The giant and Mary is good friends.
       _____

   2   The giant are very large but he are very kind.
       _____

Activity 3 Name _____

◆ The giant ◆

she

◆ Underline all the pronouns in this passage and write them in the giant's cloak. The first one has been done for you. You should find 12 different pronouns.

Mary ran very fast through the woods. <u>She</u> looked behind her to see if the giant was still following. He was. Mary was terrified. She ran faster until her sides began to ache. Suddenly she ran into the branch of a tree. It snapped in two, causing Mary to stumble. This enabled the giant to catch up.

"There you are," he said. "I have reached you at last."

"Don't come anywhere near me," Mary shrieked. "My mother and father will be here soon. Our house is just over there. They will soon sort you out!"

"But Mary, I only want to be your friend. We could have so much fun together," stammered the giant.

"Well, that is a relief," said Mary. "I thought you wanted to eat me!"

◆ These sentences are incorrect. Re-write them using correct English.

1. Mary are a good runner. She can runs very fast.

   _____

2. The giant are not mean, he want to be friends with Mary.

   _____

3. Mary and the giant is both happy now that they is friends.

   _____

Speech

Overall aims

- To reinforce understanding of speech marks – their purpose in reading and their use in writing.
- To investigate common ways of introducing and concluding dialogue.
- To collect and classify a range of dialogue functions, such as questions, statements, exclamations and orders.

Featured book

The Crazy Shoe Shuffle
by Gillian Cross

Story synopsis: It is Lee's worst day ever. First he has his football confiscated by miserable old Mr. Merton, secondly he makes his nice teacher, Miss Cherry, cross and thirdly, he is forced by his headmistress to eat his revolting school dinner. However, on the way home from school, he meets with a rather strange old lady and peculiar things begin to happen! The three teachers find themselves in the children's shoes and life as a child is not quite as pleasant as they think.

Intended learning

- To reinforce identification of speech marks and understand their purpose.
- To understand the difference between dialogue and action.

Starting point: Whole class

- Discuss the plot and the characters. What are the characters like? Is there much conversation between the characters? Does conversation give a better idea of what the characters are like?
- Read the first chapter again. How many people speak? Who speaks? How do we know when someone is speaking in a book? How is it indicated?
- Revise speech marks with the class using the board to reinforce the rule that speech marks are only placed around the words actually spoken. Use part of the text to illustrate this.
- Write some text taking out the speech marks. Is it difficult to read? Ask a child to put speech marks round the spoken words. Do the speech marks make the dialogue easier to understand?

Group activities

- Discuss with the class the scene in Chapter 2 in which Lee meets Joyce. Talk about their conversation. Put the children into pairs and ask them to role play the scene – one child taking the part of Lee, the other, Joyce. They should improvise a suitable conversation. (They do not need to use the actual words from the text.)
- Once they are happy with their conversations, ask them to write out part of the conversation using speech marks.

Plenary session

Bring the class together and ask some of the children to perform their scenes. Discuss the differences between a play and a story. Use the board to turn one of the children's writing into a piece of narrative describing the scene and conversation. Use this time to reinforce the correct punctuation to use.

Speech

◆ LESSON TWO ◆

◆ Intended learning

- To understand the purpose of speech marks and to use them in own writing.
- To investigate ways of introducing and concluding dialogue.
- To collect and use examples of dialogue functions.

◆ Starting point: Whole class

- Continue reading *The Crazy Shoe Shuffle*. Ask the children to consider how the characters are speaking. Are they asking questions? Are they shouting? Are they whispering? Muttering? Write examples from the story on the board to show the vocabulary used.
- Ask the children to experiment with speaking sentences aloud, changing their voices according to the function of the dialogue – shouting, whispering, mumbling or asking. Remind them of the punctuation associated with the function – question marks, exclamation marks and so on.

◆ Using the differentiated activity sheets

Activity sheet 1

This is aimed at children who need guidance with identifying speech within a text and who require practice in separating dialogue from action.

Activity sheet 2

This is aimed at children who are more easily able to identify speech within text and are more confident in using dialogue imaginatively.

Activity sheet 3

This is aimed at children who are easily able to identify speech in their reading and are confident in writing narrative which includes dialogue.

◆ Plenary session

For Activity sheets 1 and 2

Ask one child who worked on sheet 1 and one child who worked on sheet 2 both to explain their task to the others in the class. Ask them to read the words they put in the speech bubbles. Compare the conversations. Are they alike at all? Allow other children to contribute their ideas. Note similarities and differences.

For Activity sheets 3

Ask children working on this sheet to read aloud their story frames and compare their story lines with the original. How closely did they look at the pictures in telling their stories? Discuss the choice of 'saying' words used. Do they perform the function well?

Ask all the children to contribute appropriate 'saying' words for the dialogue.

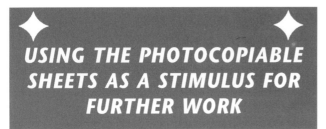

Speech

USING THE PHOTOCOPIABLE SHEETS AS A STIMULUS FOR FURTHER WORK

◆ Activity sheet 1

- What happens next? Further story frames could be added with the children's own drawings and speech bubbles.
- Further text may be written to continue the story, adding dialogue as appropriate.
- The children could highlight the words actually spoken in various ways, such as by using different colours, by underlining or by using different print.

◆ Activity sheet 2

- Suggest to the children that the speech bubble in each frame is given to the other character. For example in Frame 1, Martin speaks instead of Sarra. What could he be saying?
- Write the new conversations. Do the changes alter the plot of the story?
- On the second task on the Activity sheet, add a phrase to indicate the mood of the speaker, such as "Those boys take up the whole playground!" shouted Sarra <u>in a very cross voice</u>.

◆ Activity sheet 3

- Ask the children to add another speech bubble to the frame to extend the dialogue.
- Ask the children to draw further frames adding their own speech bubbles and text to continue the story. They could possibly add more characters.
- Suggest the children add interesting phrases to their own writing to suggest the mood of the characters such as _____, " Martin murmured sulkily.

OTHER IDEAS FOR USING SPEECH

- Use cartoons from books, magazines and newspapers and write them as dialogue.
- Suggest the children make up their own cartoon characters and story lines. Develop them into individual cartoon strips with speech bubbles.
- Make up word searches using as many 'saying' synonyms as possible.
- Brainstorm synonyms for the word *said* and collect them in a notebook or on a wallchart for future reference.
- Ask the children to tell each other 'Knock! Knock!' jokes then write them down in the form of a conversation, correctly punctuated.
- Turn a short story into a simple play and vice-versa.
- Make strips of paper with dialogue sentences written on them and further strips with words to introduce and conclude speech on them. Ask the children to pair them appropriately and write the complete sentences.
- Display basic patterns of dialogue around the room so that the rules can be referred to easily.
- Ask the children to read through stories written earlier and decide whether the word *said* could be replaced with a more effective synonym.

Grammar

KS2: Y3–4/P4–5

Activity 1   Name _____

✦ The football problem ✦

✦ Look at the pictures in the frames below. Write in the bubbles the actual words spoken by each character. Use small, neat writing.

Martin and his friends were playing football at break time. "Those boys take up the whole playground," shouted Sarra.

"It's not fair. We girls have nowhere to play," Sarra grumbled.

"It's not my fault you girls are no good at football," laughed Martin.

"Goal!" shouted Sarra. "I might let you play in my team tomorrow, Martin."

✦ Now write out the words from the speech bubbles inside the speech marks below. Remember to use only the words spoken. Underline the 'saying' word. The first has been done for you.

1 "Those boys take up the whole playground," <u>shouted</u> Sarra.
2 "..," Sarra grumbled.
3 "..," laughed Martin.
4 "..," shouted Sarra.

Grammar   Photocopiable
KS2: Y3–4/P4–5   ©Hopscotch Educational Publishing

Activity 2   **Name** _____

◆ The football problem ◆

◆ Look at the pictures in the frames below. Think what Sarra and Martin may be saying. Write their words in the bubbles. Use small, neat writing.

Martin is playing football with some other boys.

Sarra complains that the girls have nowhere to play.

Martin makes fun of Sarra.

Sarra scores a goal.

◆ Now write out the words in the speech bubbles. Make sure the speech marks are only round the words spoken. Can you change the 'said' word for a better word?

1 "..," said Sarra.
2 "..," said Sarra.
3 "..," said Martin.
4 "..," said Sarra.

Apostrophes

◆ Overall aims

- To use apostophes. To identify them in reading and understand how they are used to mark possession.
- To understand and use the term 'apostrophe' appropriately.

◆ Featured book

Bill's New Frock
by Anne Fine

Story synopsis: When Bill Simpson woke up on Monday morning, he found he was a girl. His mother dressed him in a frilly pink dress and sent him off to school. Bill soon discovers he is going to have one of the worst days of his life. Baffled by the way things are different for girls, he falls headlong into trouble, often surprising himself by the things he says and does. As the day wears on, Bill's dress becomes dirtier and tattier. His mother is appalled at the sight of him when he comes home wearily from school and Bill wonders whether he will ever return to being a boy.

◆ Intended learning

- To identify apostrophes in reading and writing and to understand how they are used to mark possession. (This is restricted to the belongings of a person only.)

◆ Starting point: Whole class

- Read the story before this lesson. Ask the children to look at the title of the book. Ask them to identify the punctuation mark (apostrophe) and ask if anyone knows why it is used. Explain that it denotes that the new frock belongs to Bill. He is the owner. Ask for examples of clothes that the children are wearing – Peter's sweater, Sally's shoes. Write the examples on the board so that the children can see just where the apostrophe should be. Restrict examples to using people's names and their belongings until the children are fully confident in the use of the apostrophe.

◆ Group activities

- Divide the class into groups and appoint a scribe. Ask the children to list characters from the book, such as Bill's classmates – Astrid, Flora, Martin, Kirsty, Philip, Talilah, Leila, Ronan, Sarah, Linda. Beside the name, ask the children to add some alliterative belongings, such as Astrid's amazing apple. These may be as amusing as they wish. Remind the children to use an apostrophe to show ownership. This activity may be extended to full sentences, alliterative or non-alliterative.

◆ Plenary session

Bring the class together to share their ideas. Ask one child to give examples of his group's answers. Write an example on the board and then turn the phrase round to form a sentence – The amazing apple is Astrid's. Ask the question, "Who does the apple belong to?" Stress the point that if something belongs to someone, the owner has the apostrophe. Take time to give plenty of examples. It is important that the children fully grasp the concept at this stage so that they will less easily misplace the apostrophe when dealing with more complicated examples of possessive apostrophes in the future.

Apostrophes

LESSON TWO

◆ Intended learning

✦ To further understand the use of the apostrophe and to make use of it in own writing.

◆ Starting point: Whole class

✦ Review the work of the previous lesson reminding the class of the need for an apostrophe for an owner of belongings. Ask the class to be aware of the need for apostrophes in the text. Write some examples of possession on the board in which the belongings are plural, such as *The teacher's comics* or *Bill's pencils*. Explain that the apostrophe is always placed with the owner not the belongings. Turn the phrase round to give further emphasis – 'The comics belonging to the teacher' and 'The pencils belonging to Bill'. It is important that the children understand this concept to avoid the problem of putting apostrophes in plurals. At this stage do not attempt to teach the rules for plural owners (The teachers' comics). Give plenty of examples for the children to practise.

◆ Using the differentiated activity sheets

Activity sheet 1

This is aimed at children who need basic practice in the use of the apostrophe for possession.

Activity sheet 2

This is aimed at children who are more confident in applying their understanding of the apostrophe.

Activity sheet 3

This is aimed at children who are quite confident in using the apostrophe. It also gives scope for personal and imaginative writing.

◆ Plenary session

For Activity sheet 1

Ask one child to pair up the belongings with the owners and read aloud their sentences. Check that the others agree. Ask for examples of the children's own sentences. Are the belongings appropriate to the owners?

For Activity sheet 2

Ask one child to read aloud some of his sentences. Write examples on the board to remind the class of where the apostrophe should be. Refer to the exercise in which the apostrophes are misplaced. Ask why they cannot be put in these places. Is there an owner for each one? Remind the class that the apostrophe goes with the owner and not the item/belonging.

For Activity sheet 3

Ask some children to read their passages and their continuing stories. Discuss the use of the apostrophe in both the exercise and the story continuation.

Grammar
KS2: Y3–4/P4–5

Activity 1   Name _____

◆ Bill runs an errand ◆

◆ Bill's teacher asks him to go to the school office. On the way he meets people who ask him to take items to the office. Here are pictures of people in the school and their belongings.

   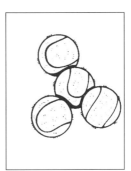 

◆ Pair the people with their belongings. Underline the owner and put an apostrophe after the owner's name. The first has been done for you.

1 The <u>teacher</u>'s key   2 ....

3 ....   4 ....

5 ....   6 ....

◆ Write each one a different way. The first has been done for you.

1 *The key belongs to the teacher. It is the teacher's key.*

2 ....

3 ....

4 ....

5 ....

6 ....

Grammar

KS2: Y3–4/P4–5

Photocopiable

©Hopscotch Educational Publishing

49

Activity 2 Name _____

✦ Bill runs an errand ✦

✦ Bill has been asked to take some items to the school office. Draw a line to match the items with the correct person.

the teacher	a computer
the caretaker	a key
the headteacher	medical notes
the nurse	tennis balls
the secretary	the register

✦ Write a phrase to show which item belongs to each person. Use an apostrophe. The first has been done for you.

1 *The secretary's computer*..
2 ....
3 ....
4 ....
5 ....

✦ Now add some words to make each a complete sentence. For example: *The secretary's computer stood on her desk in the office.*

✦ In the following sentences, the apostrophes have been put in the wrong place. Correct the sentences.

1 Bills dress was very pretty but it had no pocket's.
2 Mrs Bandarainas office was up the stair's and along the corridor.
3 Bill dropped the caretakers tennis ball's just as he got to the office.

Activity 3

◆ Bill runs an errand ◆

◆ Put the apostrophes in the following passage.

Bill was very happy that he was chosen to take the teachers key back to the office.

"Just take the key to Mrs. Bandarainas office," said Mrs. Collins, "and hurry back."

Bill was pleased to get out of the classroom and dawdled along the corridors. Suddenly he met the headmaster.

The headmaster put his hand on Bills head. "Are you going to the office?" he asked. "Do me a favour and take these coloured inks to Mrs. Bandarainas office. Don't drop them!"

So Bill picked up the headmasters ink bottles, put them with the teachers key and went on.

At the top of the stairs the school nurse met him. "Just what I need. Someone who can take these medical forms to Mrs Bandarainas office," she said. "Don't drop them!"

So Bill carried the nurses medical notes with the headmasters inks and the teachers key and once more set off for the office. He thought he would put the inks and the key in his pocket, but Bills frock had no pockets, so he had to carry them.

Just then he heard a rapping on the window. Outside stood the caretaker. He leaned through the window.

He said, "Off to Mrs Bandarainas office are you? Just take these tennis balls with you and ask her to lock them away."

Before Bill could argue, the caretakers tennis balls were put in his arms.

Very carefully he made his way to Mrs. Bandarainas office, carrying the teachers key, the headmasters inks, the nurses medical notes and the caretakers tennis balls.

"Mind you don't spill the ink on that sweet little frock," said Mrs Bandaraina.

It wasn't Bills fault. His hands began to shake he was so cross. Suddenly the whole lot crashed to the floor!

◆ You should have put in 19 apostrophes.

◆ What happened next? Continue the story on the back of this sheet. Remember to use apostrophes where necessary.

Sentence length

◆ Overall aims

- To explore ways of shortening sentences by deletion.
- To explore words which carry most meaning in sentences.
- To investigate through reading and writing how ideas can be joined in complex ways through using a wide range of conjunctions.

◆ Featured book

The Chocolate Touch
by Patrick Skeyne Catling

Story synopsis: John Midas is quite an ordinary boy except he has one bad fault. He is a pig about sweets – toffees, lollipops, peppermints, Turkish delight – and above all, chocolate. He devours them all. It is his greed for sweets which leads him to buy a very special box of chocolates. The box only contains one chocolate but it leaves him with a gift that could be a dream come true - or a nightmare. Everything he touches turns to chocolate.

◆ Intended learning

- To identify key words, phrases or sentences in reading – those that carry most meaning.
- To understand that some words are more essential to meaning than others.
- To explore ways of shortening sentences by deletion.

◆ Starting point: Whole class

- Read the blurb on the back cover of the book to the children. Ask them if they know the purpose of the blurb. Read blurbs of other familiar books. Discuss the purpose of giving a brief summary of the story.
- Ask the children to think about the main ideas in the story (the plot). Discuss the characters and the plot. Explain to the children that they are going to produce a class summary of Chapter 2. Read this chapter and ask for the main ideas. Ask the children to decide which parts of the chapter are important and which are not so important to the plot. Discuss why. Write their suggestions for the main ideas on the board. These should be used to write a short summary.
- Explain to the children that some words in sentences are more important than others to give meaning. Give some examples from the text and discuss which words are most important.

◆ Group activities

- Working in pairs, give the children a number of sentences from the story. One child in the pair must underline what s/he considers to be the key words in each sentence. The child then gives his/her partner only those key words and his partner has to make up his own sentences using those words. They should then compare the sentences with the original. Do they carry similar meanings?

◆ Plenary session

Bring the class together to discuss their work. Discuss the words they thought carried most meaning in the sentences. What sort of words were they? Was it necessary to underline a verb? A noun? Which words did they think were more important and least important in a sentence? Discuss how we could use important words, such as in notes, headlines and titles. Discuss examples.

Sentence length

◆ LESSON TWO ◆

◆ Intended learning

- To investigate through reading and writing how ideas can be joined in more complex ways through a widening range of conjunctions.
- To understand and use the term 'conjunction'.

◆ Starting point: Whole class

- Review the previous lesson by discussing how sentences can be shortened and why it is sometimes necessary to shorten them. Then explain that sometimes sentences need to be made longer and more complex. A series of short sentences can give stilted reading and writing so to create fluency some sentences may need to be extended.
- Use the sentences from *The Chocolate Touch* as a basis for the following exercise. Write some examples of short sentences on the board. Ask the children to suggest ways in which the sentences can be linked to create one sentence containing two ideas. For example, 'John went to a local school. He usually liked it.' The obvious joining word is *and*. Write other sentences so that a variety of conjunctions may be suggested, such as *but, then, because, so* and *as*. Decide whether the choice of conjunction can alter the meaning of the sentence. For example, 'John left the sweetshop after the shopkeeper had given him the chocolates.' or 'John left the sweetshop before the shopkeeper had given him the chocolates.'

◆ Using the differentiated activity sheets

Activity sheet 1

This is for children who need guidance in choosing the most appropriate conjunction in their writing. The task also gives practice in combining two ideas in a sentence with the use of a conjunction.

Activity sheet 2

This is for children who need less guidance in the choice of a suitable conjunction and who are able to experiment with using their own in their writing.

Activity sheet 3

This is aimed at children who are confident in using conjunctions and will enjoy experimenting with them.

◆ Plenary session

For Activity sheet 1

Ask one child to read the sentences with the correct conjunction. Ask if the others agree. Could alternative conjunctions have been used? Ask for some examples of the children's own sentences. Do they make sense?

For Activity sheet 2

Ask one child to read his/her version of the passage. Compare it with another child's work. Are the children using the same conjunction in each case? Does the passage still make sense if an alternative conjunction is used? This exercise should indicate to children that there is not always a single correct answer.

For Activity sheet 3

One or two of these children could read out their passages. The other children should listen for differences between them. They will be slightly different to allow for personal choice. Then enjoy sharing the 'excuses' with the class.

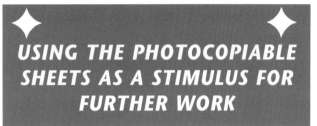

Sentence length

USING THE PHOTOCOPIABLE SHEETS AS A STIMULUS FOR FURTHER WORK

- Some children could take the joining of sentences one step further by joining three simple sentences with conjunctions.

- Others could use the passage on Activity sheet 3 as an exercise in shortening (summarising) a passage. They should decide upon the important ideas and words and use them to reduce the text to 50–60 words.

- Make up 'Excuse' poems on a variety of subjects, such as 'Why I was late for school' or 'Why I didn't tidy my bedroom'. Suggest a variety of conjunctions which may be used.

- Write a story in which they have a craving for chocolate. What happens?

- Ask the children to write a newspaper report about 'Janice's problem'. They should conduct an interview with her. Alternatively they could make a tape recording of an interview.

OTHER IDEAS FOR SENTENCE LENGTH

- Give the children a passage of text in which the words 'and' and 'then' are overused. Ask them to proof read the passage suggesting alternative conjunctions or shortening the sentences by using full stops.

- Brainstorm conjunctions with the class and try to make an alphabetical list of them for display and for future reference.

- Give the children newspaper articles and ask them to make up suitable headlines for each article.

- Give the children some examples of poetry and ask them to underline the most important or most effective words in each line. Ask them to explain the importance.

- Ask the children to make as many different sentences as possible by keeping the main sentence but altering the conjunction. For example, 'The boys left the playground _____ the girls were there. Conjunctions that could be used are: *because, as, since, while, if, until* and *although*. This task can illustrate clearly how the use of a conjunction can alter the meaning of a sentence.

Activity 1   **Name** _____

◆ Chocolate delight! ◆

✦ Choose the correct conjunction to join these sentences. Write out the sentence you have made.

1 Janice loves chocolate. It tastes so good. (because, and)
   _____

2 She loves all kinds of chocolate. Chocolate milk shakes are her favourite. (as, but)
   _____
   _____

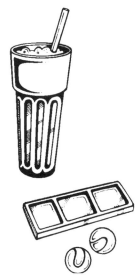

3 Janice could eat chocolate for breakfast. She could eat it for lunch and dinner too! (and, however)
   _____

4 One day she was very ill. Her mother phoned the doctor. (but, so)
   _____

5 The doctor examined Janice. Her mother held her hand. (however, while)
   _____

6 The doctor ordered her to stop eating chocolate. She felt better. (whenever, until)
   _____

✦ Complete the sentences below so they make sense. Underline the conjunctions.

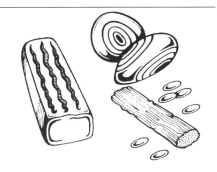

1 Janice said, "I love chocolate because _____

2 She saves up all her money until _____

3 She is allowed to eat chocolate at home but _____
   _____

Grammar   Photocopiable

Activity 2   Name _____

✦ Chocolate delight! ✦

✦ Choose a suitable conjunction from the box to write in the spaces.

unless	but	since	as	however	until	for
since	so	if	yet	because	while	
before	when	and	though	then		

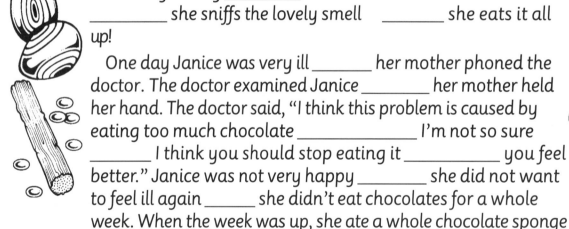

Janice Bean just loves chocolate! She loves it _____ it tastes so good. She loves all kinds of chocolate _____ chocolate milk shakes are her favourite. Janice could eat chocolate for breakfast _____ she could eat it for lunch and dinner too! She saves up all her money _____ she has enough to buy a tasty treat. She hides them in her room _____ she takes them out one by one. She likes to unwrap them very slowly _____ all the chocolate is bare _____ she sniffs the lovely smell _____ she eats it all up!

One day Janice was very ill _____ her mother phoned the doctor. The doctor examined Janice _____ her mother held her hand. The doctor said, "I think this problem is caused by eating too much chocolate _____ I'm not so sure _____ I think you should stop eating it _____ you feel better." Janice was not very happy _____ she did not want to feel ill again _____ she didn't eat chocolates for a whole week. When the week was up, she ate a whole chocolate sponge cake! What a chocolate delight!

✦ Which conjunctions did you **not** use? Make up some sentences of your own using these conjunctions. Write them here:

Activity 3   Name _____

◆ Chocolate delight! ◆

◆ Some of these sentences are too short. Proof read the passage and choose conjunctions from the box to join the sentences.

unless	but	since	as	however	until	whenever
since	so	if	yet	because	for	while	before
when	and		though	then	although	

Janice Bean just loves chocolate! She loves it. It tastes so good. She loves all kinds of chocolate. Chocolate milk shakes are her favourite. Janice could eat chocolate for breakfast. She could eat it for lunch and dinner too! She saves up all her money until she has enough to buy a tasty treat. She hides them in her room. She takes them out one by one. She likes to unwrap them very slowly until all the chocolate is bare. She sniffs the lovely smell. She eats it all up!

One day Janice was very ill. Her mother phoned the doctor. The doctor examined Janice. Her mother held her hand. The doctor said, "I think this problem is caused by eating too much chocolate. I'm not so sure. I think you should stop eating it until you feel better." Janice was not very happy. She did not want to feel ill again. She didn't eat chocolates for a whole week. When the week was up, she ate a whole chocolate sponge cake! What a chocolate delight!

◆ Re-read through your work carefully. Do all the sentences make sense?

◆ Now make up some excuses that Janice might have given to the doctor for eating so much chocolate. Try to make your excuses original and amusing!

1 I must eat lots of chocolate because _____

2 I would eat less chocolate but _____

Grammar   Photocopiable

Using paragraphs

◆ Overall aims

- To identify paragraphs in reading and investigate how they are used to organise ideas.
- To understand and use the term 'paragraph'.
- To use paragraphs to organise/reorganise own writing.

◆ Featured book

Charlotte's Web
by E B White

Story synopsis: This is the story of a little girl named Fern who loved a little pig named Wilbur. Wilbur's dear friend Charlotte, a beautiful grey spider, saves Wilbur from the usual fate of nice fat pigs by a wonderfully clever plan which no one else could possibly have thought of. There are many other interesting characters on Mr. Zuckerman's farm – a grey rat called Templeton, an irresponsible goose and many more. This story is especially good for reading aloud.

◆ LESSON ONE ◆

◆ Intended learning

- To understand the term 'paragraph'.
- To investigate the purpose of paragraphing in reading and writing.

◆ Starting point: Whole class

- Ask the children to share their ideas about the plot and the characters. Talk about the layout of the book, for example that there are 22 chapters each with a chapter heading. Ask the children why they think each chapter has a title. What job does the title do? Why are books divided up into chapters? Do chapters make reading a book easier? Introduce the concept of each chapter being divided up into paragraphs. What is a paragraph? What is its job? Does separating text into paragraphs make for easier reading?
- Look at other books to see how they are written in chapters with paragraphs. Ask the children if they can identify why a new paragraph is used. Collect as many instances as possible, for example when a person speaks, to introduce a new time, a new character, a new place or a change of subject.
- If possible reproduce a page or two from the book and study it with the children discussing why the writer decided to begin new paragraphs.

◆ Group activities

- Divide the children into groups. Give each group a piece of round paper to represent a spider's body. Write a 'main idea' sentence on the 'body'. For example, 'It was the day that Wilbur met Charlotte for the first time.' Give the groups eight strips of paper to represent the spider's legs. Ask the children to each write on the strips sentences about the main idea. For example, 'She looked up and saw a giant cobweb in the corner.' Ask them to arrange the 'legs' in a suitable order around the body. This task helps children to understand how a paragraph usually has a main sentence followed by relevant detail.

◆ Plenary session

Bring the class together again to share their ideas. Use one group's spider as an example and reproduce it on the board. Discuss the detail sentences. Do they make sense? Are they relevant to the main idea? Discuss the order of the sentences. Should any changes be made? Write the paragraph on the board and discuss indentation as a way of clearly indicating a new paragraph. Discuss whether the paragraph is too long or needs more additions.

Using paragraphs

◆ LESSON TWO ◆

◆ Intended learning

◆ To use paragraphs to organise written text.

◆ Starting point: Whole class

◆ Make a whole class summary or synopsis of the book. Ask the children to suggest the main ideas in the story. Use these as paragraph titles. Decide upon the order of the paragraphs and write them on the board. Ask the children for some detail sentences about each paragraph and write them under each paragraph title. Decide on a suitable order for the sentences. Put the paragraphs together to create a whole class synopsis. Explain to the children that using paragraphs is a sensible way of organising ideas and events in a story.

◆ Using the differentiated activity sheets

Explain to the children that they will have the opportunity of using paragraphs to organise their own writing.

Activity sheet 1

This is aimed at children who need practice in investigating how paragraphs are used in breaking up a long piece of writing.

Activity sheet 2

This is aimed at children who are more confident in identifying the need for paragraphs but who need practice in organising their paragraphs.

Activity sheet 3

This is aimed at children who are beginning to write accurately in paragraphs and can organise their work more effectively.

◆ Plenary session

When the children have completed their activity sheets, bring the class together to discuss their work.

For Activity sheet 1

Ask one child to read aloud each paragraph and give his/her titles for them. Do the others agree that the titles are relevant? Could they suggest any improvements? Discuss the number of sentences in each paragraph.

For Activity sheet 2

Ask one child to read his/her work. Do the others agree that the paragraphs have been put in the correct order? Ask for some examples of 'What happened next?' paragraphs.

For Activity sheet 3

Ask one child to indicate where s/he demarked her/his paragraphs. Could they be in different places? Discuss examples of the extra four paragraphs written by these children. Are they relevant? Interesting? Amusing? How did the stories end?

Grammar

KS2: Y3–4/P4–5

Using paragraphs

USING THE PHOTOCOPIABLE SHEETS AS A STIMULUS FOR FURTHER WORK

- Ask the children to look at the Activity sheets and explain why the writer started a new paragraph in each instance. Was there a change of person? A change of time? Speaker? By identifying why authors start new paragraphs, the children will become more familiar with their use and more confident in using them in their own writing.

- Ask the children to write a story in which they have been given a pet for a present. What pet would they choose?

- Suggest the children research cats in the library. Ask them to find out as many facts as they can. You may wish to suggest areas of research. Ask them to write a factual account about cats. Encourage the children to use paragraphs to separate their text into subject areas.

- The above exercise could be carried out using spiders as the topic for research.

- In the book, Fern has to look after her pet pig. Ask the children to either write a list of instructions on how to look after a pig or instructions on how to look after a pet of their choice.

OTHER IDEAS FOR USING PARAGRAPHS

- Encourage the children to use flow diagrams to help organise their work into paragraphs. This is especially useful when writing factual accounts.

- Ask the children to proof read some of their own writing or a partner's work and put it into paragraphs where needed.

- Give the children a list of simple instructions, such as for making a cup of tea. Ask them to add detail by making paragraphs for each instruction. For example, Warm the pot – the children will need to explain exactly how to warm the pot.

- Give the children plenty of practice in extracting the main or important sentences from paragraphs in factual accounts. This gives good practice in extracting relevant detail for comprehension exercises and in researching topics in other areas of the curriculum. It is also valuable as an exercise in summarising accounts.

- Ask the children to write descriptions of themselves. They should suggest ideas for paragraph headings, such as face and expressions, clothes and so on.

- When the children are asked to write a story, give them a choice of two or three opening paragraphs and two or three closing paragraphs. They must choose one from each and add three or four paragraphs of their own in between. This task gives good practice in story planning.

- The use of a word processor is a valuable tool in ordering paragraphs in both narrative and factual writing.

Activity 1   Name _____

✦ The birthday surprise ✦

✦ Read the following passage carefully.

Nareeta woke up. It was her birthday but she did not feel very happy because she had asked for a kitten for her birthday and her father had said that she couldn't have one.

   Nareeta got up, had a wash and went downstairs. She went into the kitchen to find lots of presents waiting for her.

   "Oh, thank you Mum and Dad, these are lovely," she said as she opened each present one by one, then sat down to eat her breakfast.

   "Haven't you forgotten something?" asked Dad. "Look on the floor."

   Nareeta looked down and saw a large box, tied up with a huge bow. She carefully opened it and there inside was the most gorgeous kitten she had ever seen!

   "Oh, thank you, thank you," she cried with delight, "I'm the happiest person alive!"

✦ Answer these questions:

How many paragraphs are there? ☐

How many sentences are there in the first paragraph? ☐

How many sentences in the last paragraph? ☐

Which paragraph tells us that Nareeta got a kitten for her birthday? ☐

Which paragraph tells us that Nareeta was not happy when she woke up? ☐

✦ Write a sentence to give each paragraph a title.

1 _____
2 _____
3 _____
4 _____
5 _____
6 _____

Grammar   Photocopiable

Activity 2   Name _____

◆ The birthday surprise ◆

✦ The six paragraphs in the story below are in the wrong order. Cut them out and put them in the correct order. To help you, a title is given for each paragraph.

Paragraph titles:
Nareeta wakes up on her birthday.
Nareeta goes down to the kitchen.
Nareeta thanks her parents for her presents.
Dad asks her to look on the floor.
Nareeta opens a box with a kitten inside it.
Nareeta is very happy about her birthday surprise.

"Oh, thank you Mum and Dad, these are lovely," she said as she opened each present one by one, then sat down to eat her breakfast.

Nareeta woke up. It was her birthday but she did not feel very happy because she had asked for a kitten for her birthday and her father had said that she couldn't have one.

"Oh, thank you, thank you," she cried with delight, "I'm the happiest person alive!"

Nareeta got up, had a wash and went downstairs. She went into the kitchen to find lots of presents waiting for her.

Nareeta looked down and saw a large box, tied up with a huge bow. She carefully opened it and there inside was the most gorgeous kitten she had ever seen!

"Haven't you forgotten something?" asked Dad. "Look on the floor."

✦ When you are happy with the order of your paragraphs, glue them onto another sheet of paper. Now write another paragraph of your own to say what you think happened next. Write a sentence title for your paragraph.

Activity 3　　　　　　　　　　　　　　　　　　Name _____

◆ The birthday surprise ◆

◆ Divide the passage below into 6 paragraphs by using the mark //. The first one has been done for you.

Nareeta wakes up on her birthday

Nareeta goes down to the kitchen

Nareeta thanks her parents for her presents

Dad asks her to look on the floor

Nareeta opens a box with a kitten inside it.

Nareeta is very happy about her birthday surprise.

Nareeta lifts the kitten out and feeds it some warm milk.

Together, the family decide on a name for the kitten.

Nareeta takes the kitten outside.

A dog appears and frightens the kitten.

Nareeta woke up. It was her birthday but she did not feel very happy because she had asked for a kitten for her birthday and her father had said that she couldn't have one. // Nareeta got up, had a wash and went downstairs. She went into the kitchen to find lots of presents waiting for her. "Oh, thank you Mum and Dad, these are lovely," she said as she opened each present one by one, then sat down to eat her breakfast. "Haven't you forgotten something?" asked Dad. "Look on the floor." Nareeta looked down and saw a large box, tied up with a huge bow. She carefully opened it and there inside was the most gorgeous kitten she had ever seen! "Oh, thank you, thank you," she cried with delight, "I'm the happiest person alive!"

◆ Continue the story using the paragraph titles:

◆ Decide how the story ends. Complete the story on the back of this page. Remember to use paragraphs.

Acknowledgements

The following is a list of all the children's storybooks that have been referred to in this book as the basis for grammar work.

- ***The Hodgeheg*** by Dick King-Smith (Puffin)
- ***The Better Brown Stories*** by Allan Ahlberg (Puffin)
- ***The BFG*** by Roald Dahl (Puffin)
- ***Charlotte's Web*** by E B White (Puffin)
- ***The Crazy Shoe Shuffle*** by Gillian Cross (Mammoth)
- ***Bill's New Frock*** by Anne Fine (Mammoth)
- ***The Chocolate Touch*** by Patrick Skeyne Catling (Mammoth)
- ***The Iron Man*** by Ted Hughes (Faber & Faber)
- ***The Hobbit*** by J R R Tolkien (Unwin)
- ***The Suitcase Kid*** by Jacqueline Wilson (Yearling)